CONGRATULATIONS ON YOUR GRADUATION

summersdale

CONRATULATIONS ON YOUR GRADUATION

First published in 2020

An Hachette UK Company
www.hachette.co.uk

Summersdale Publishers
Part of Octopus Publishing Group Limited
Carmelite House
50 Victoria Embankment
LONDON
EC4Y 0DZ
UK

www.summersdale.com

This FSC® label means that materials used for the product have been responsibly sourced

MIX
Paper | Supporting responsible forestry
FSC www.fsc.org
FSC® C016973

The authorized representative in the EEA is Hachette Ireland, 8 Castlecourt Centre, Dublin 15, D15 XTP3, Ireland (email: info@hbgi.ie)

Printed and bound in China

ISBN: 978-1-83799-609-4

TO..............................

FROM.........................

MY DEAR,
TERRIFIED GRADUATES,
YOU ARE ABOUT TO ENTER
THE MOST UNCERTAIN
AND THRILLING PERIOD
OF YOUR LIVES.

LIN-MANUEL MIRANDA

I WAS SMART ENOUGH TO GO THROUGH ANY DOOR THAT OPENED.

JOAN RIVERS

CAPS OFF TO YOU!

YOUR EDUCATION IS A DRESS REHEARSAL FOR A LIFE THAT IS YOURS TO LEAD.

NORA EPHRON

WHAT WE
LEARN WITH
PLEASURE
WE NEVER
FORGET.

ALFRED MERCIER

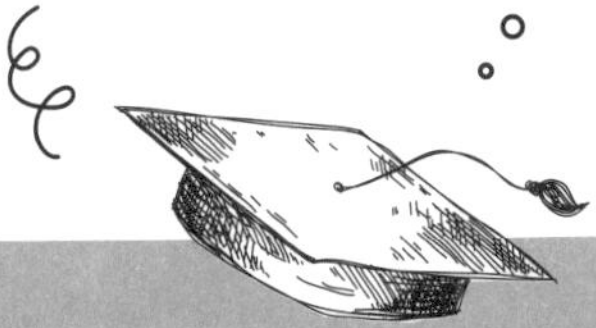

STEP INTO THE
NEW STORY YOU
ARE WILLING
TO CREATE.

OPRAH WINFREY

THE
ADVENTURE
STARTS
HERE

DON'T JUST GET INVOLVED. FIGHT FOR YOUR SEAT AT THE TABLE. BETTER YET, FIGHT FOR A SEAT AT THE HEAD OF THE TABLE.

BARACK OBAMA

SUCCESS IS NEVER FINAL. FAILURE IS NEVER FATAL. IT'S COURAGE THAT COUNTS.

ANONYMOUS

YOU

DID IT!

THERE ARE
FAR, FAR BETTER
THINGS AHEAD
THAN ANY WE
LEAVE BEHIND.

C. S. LEWIS

Your life is your story, and the adventure ahead of you is the journey to fulfil your own purpose and potential.

KERRY WASHINGTON

CHAMPIONS ARE MADE FROM SOMETHING THEY HAVE DEEP INSIDE THEM – A DESIRE, A DREAM, A VISION.

MUHAMMAD ALI

BOUNCE BACK FROM EVERY "NO" AND YOU'LL FIND THE BEST "YES"

THERE IS
NO SCRIPT.
LIVE YOUR LIFE.
SOAK IT ALL IN.

DICK COSTOLO

IF YOU'RE NOT MAKING SOME NOTABLE MISTAKES ALONG THE WAY, YOU'RE CERTAINLY NOT TAKING ENOUGH BUSINESS AND CAREER CHANCES.

SALLIE KRAWCHECK

Dare to

DREAM BIG

THE OLD RULES
ARE CRUMBLING AND NOBODY
KNOWS WHAT THE NEW RULES ARE.
SO MAKE UP YOUR OWN RULES.

NEIL GAIMAN

THERE IS
NO WAY TO
SHORT-CIRCUIT
THE PATH TO
SUCCESS.

TORY BURCH

THE WORLD OF
THE FUTURE IS
IN OUR MAKING.
TOMORROW
IS NOW.

ELEANOR ROOSEVELT

THERE ARE ENDLESS DOORS OPEN BEFORE YOU

EDUCATION IS ONE OF THE BLESSINGS OF LIFE – AND ONE OF ITS NECESSITIES.

MALALA YOUSAFZAI

AN INVESTMENT IN KNOWLEDGE PAYS THE BEST INTEREST.

BENJAMIN FRANKLIN

EVERY ACHIEVEMENT STARTS WITH THE MOTIVATION TO BEGIN

I used to want the words
"She tried" on my tombstone.
Now I want "She did it".

KATHERINE DUNHAM

I CHOOSE TO MAKE
THE REST OF MY LIFE
THE BEST OF MY LIFE.

LOUISE HAY

GIVE IT YOUR ALL.
DARE TO BE ALL
YOU CAN BE.

HILLARY CLINTON

THE
WORLD IS YOUR
OYSTER

DON'T LET THE NOISE
OF OTHERS' OPINIONS DROWN
OUT YOUR OWN INNER VOICE...
HAVE THE COURAGE TO
FOLLOW YOUR HEART
AND INTUITION.

STEVE JOBS

IF YOU
DON'T RISK
ANYTHING,
YOU RISK
EVEN MORE.

ERICA JONG

DON'T LOOK BACK – YOU AREN'T GOING THAT WAY

SUCCESS USUALLY COMES TO THOSE WHO ARE TOO BUSY TO BE LOOKING FOR IT.

HENRY DAVID THOREAU

START WHERE YOU ARE. USE WHAT YOU HAVE. DO WHAT YOU CAN.

ARTHUR ASHE

DON'T BE AFRAID OF FEAR. BECAUSE IT SHARPENS YOU, IT CHALLENGES YOU, IT MAKES YOU STRONGER.

ED HELMS

Anything

IS POSSIBLE

THE HIGHEST RESULT OF EDUCATION IS TOLERANCE.

HELEN KELLER

Education is our passport to the future, for tomorrow belongs to the people who preparefor it today.

MALCOLM X

WHATEVER
YOU WANT,
START
WORKING
TOWARD
IT TODAY

THE ROAD LESS
TRAVELED IS SOMETIMES
FRAUGHT WITH BARRICADES,
BUMPS, AND UNCHARTED TERRAIN.
BUT IT IS ON THAT ROAD
WHERE YOUR CHARACTER
IS TRULY TESTED.

KATIE COURIC

SELF-TRUST IS
THE FIRST SECRET
OF SUCCESS.

RALPH WALDO EMERSON

TRY NOT TO BECOME
A MAN OF SUCCESS,
BUT RATHER BECOME
A MAN OF VALUE.

ALBERT EINSTEIN

YOU'RE ONE
STEP CLOSER
TO FINDING OUT
WHO YOU'RE
GOING TO BE

GO INTO THE WORLD AND DO WELL. BUT MORE IMPORTANTLY, GO INTO THE WORLD AND DO GOOD.

MINOR MYERS JR

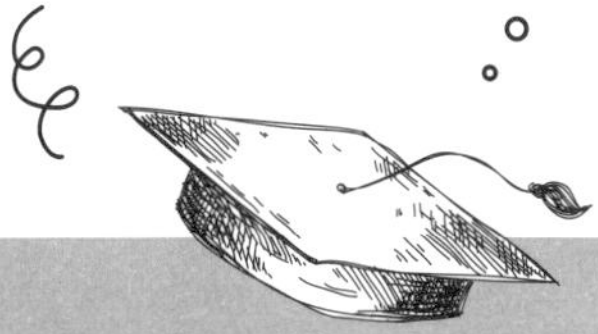

NOW THAT YOU'VE GRADUATED, JUST REMEMBER: BOSSES DON'T USUALLY ACCEPT NOTES FROM YOUR MOTHER.

MELANIE WHITE

YOU
CAN AND
YOU WILL

IF YOU DON'T
LIKE THE ROAD
YOU'RE WALKING,
START PAVING
ANOTHER ONE.

DOLLY PARTON

GRADUATION IS A PROCESS
THAT GOES ON UNTIL THE
LAST DAY OF YOUR LIFE.
IF YOU CAN GRASP THAT,
YOU'LL MAKE A DIFFERENCE.

ARIE PENCOVICI

THE ESSENCE
OF KNOWLEDGE
IS, HAVING IT, TO
APPLY IT. NOT
HAVING IT, TO
CONFESS YOUR
IGNORANCE.

CONFUCIUS

SEIZE THE DAY,
EVERY DAY, AND
YOU WILL SEIZE
YOUR DREAMS

I'M NOT TELLING YOU
IT'S GOING TO BE EASY.
I'M TELLING YOU IT'S
GOING TO BE WORTH IT.

ART WILLIAMS JR

You can never leave footprints that last if you are always walking on tiptoe.

LEYMAH GBOWEE

Con-grad

-ULATIONS!

INTELLIGENCE PLUS CHARACTER – THAT IS THE GOAL OF TRUE EDUCATION.

MARTIN LUTHER KING JR

ACCEPT RESPONSIBILITY
FOR YOUR LIFE. KNOW THAT
IT IS YOU WHO WILL GET YOU
WHERE YOU WANT TO GO,
NO ONE ELSE.

LES BROWN

A DREAM
DOES NOT
BECOME REALITY
THROUGH MAGIC.
IT TAKES SWEAT,
DETERMINATION
AND HARD WORK.

COLIN POWELL

IT JUST GOT ONE DEGREE HOTTER!

THE MERE FACT OF BEING ABLE TO CALL YOUR JOB YOUR PASSION IS SUCCESS IN MY EYES.

ALICIA VIKANDER

DOUBT KILLS
MORE DREAMS
THAN FAILURE
EVER WILL.

SUZY KASSEM

GOOD THINGS COME TO THOSE WHO **WORK** FOR THEM!

AT COMMENCEMENT
YOU WEAR YOUR SQUARE-
SHAPED MORTAR BOARDS.
MY HOPE IS THAT FROM TIME
TO TIME YOU WILL LET YOUR
MINDS BE BOLD, AND
WEAR SOMBREROS.

PAUL FREUND

THE FIRST
OF MANY
GRADUATIONS
IN LIFE. EACH
ONE HOLDS
SUCCESSES FOR
YOU TO ENJOY.

CATHERINE PULSIFER

There are many things that seem impossible only so long as one does not attempt them.

ANDRÉ GIDE

YOUR EDUCATION IS SOMETHING YOU CAN NEVER LOSE

WINNERS TAKE TIME
TO RELISH THEIR WORK...
SCALING THE MOUNTAIN IS
WHAT MAKES THE VIEW FROM
THE TOP SO EXHILARATING.

DENIS WAITLEY

DO NOT WAIT
TO STRIKE TILL
THE IRON IS HOT;
BUT MAKE IT HOT
BY STRIKING.

BENJAMIN FRANKLIN

DEFINE
SUCCESS FOR
YOURSELF

ONCE IN A RARE WHILE,
SOMEBODY COMES ALONG WHO
DOESN'T JUST RAISE THE BAR,
THEY CREATE AN ENTIRELY NEW
STANDARD OF MEASUREMENT.

DICK COSTOLO

TO ACCOMPLISH GREAT THINGS, WE MUST NOT ONLY ACT, BUT ALSO DREAM, NOT ONLY PLAN, BUT ALSO BELIEVE.

ANATOLE FRANCE

LIFE SHRINKS
OR EXPANDS IN
PROPORTION TO
ONE'S COURAGE.

ANAÏS NIN

This is just the

BEGINNING

RESULTS HAPPEN
OVER TIME,
NOT OVERNIGHT.
WORK HARD, STAY
CONSISTENT, AND
BE PATIENT.

ANONYMOUS

FIGHT FOR WHAT MAKES YOU OPTIMISTIC ABOUT THE WORLD. FIND IT, INSIST ON IT, DIG INTO IT, GO AFTER IT.

JENNIFER GARNER

THERE'S NO STOPPING YOU NOW!

YOU CAN'T CLIMB THE LADDER OF SUCCESS WITH YOUR HANDS IN YOUR POCKETS.

ARNOLD SCHWARZENEGGER

The more that you read,
the more things you will know.
The more that you learn,
the more places you'll go.

DR SEUSS

DO NOT FOLLOW WHERE THE PATH MAY LEAD. GO INSTEAD WHERE THERE IS NO PATH AND LEAVE A TRAIL.

RALPH WALDO EMERSON

UNLEASH YOUR POTENTIAL

THERE ARE NO REGRETS IN LIFE. JUST LESSONS.

JENNIFER ANISTON

YOU CANNOT DREAM OF BECOMING SOMETHING YOU DO NOT KNOW ABOUT. YOU HAVE TO LEARN TO DREAM BIG. EDUCATION EXPOSES US TO WHAT THE WORLD HAS TO OFFER.

SONIA SOTOMAYOR

THE HARDER
THE BATTLE,
THE SWEETER
THE VICTORY

TO TRAVEL
HOPEFULLY IS
A BETTER THING
THAN TO ARRIVE,
AND THE TRUE
SUCCESS IS
TO LABOR.

ROBERT LOUIS STEVENSON

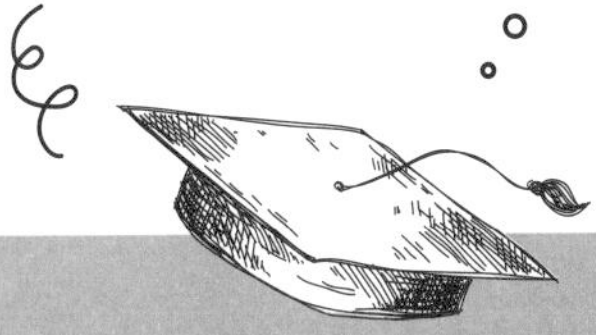

THE FUTURE CANNOT BE PREDICTED, BUT FUTURES CAN BE INVENTED.

DENNIS GABOR

KNOWLEDGE
IS NOT POWER.
IT IS THE
IMPLEMENTATION
OF KNOWLEDGE
THAT IS POWER.

LARRY WINGET

WHEN YOU
BECOME
FEARLESS,
LIFE BECOMES
LIMITLESS

DON'T EVER UNDERESTIMATE
THE IMPORTANCE YOU CAN HAVE,
BECAUSE HISTORY HAS SHOWN
US THAT COURAGE CAN BE
CONTAGIOUS AND HOPE CAN
TAKE ON A LIFE OF ITS OWN.

MICHELLE OBAMA

BE THE HARDEST WORKING PERSON YOU KNOW. BECAUSE IF YOU'RE NOT, SOMEONE ELSE WILL BE.

IAN BRENNAN

Be a TRAILBLAZER

You will stumble and fall; you will experience both disaster and triumph, sometimes in the same day. But... neither triumphs nor disasters last forever.

HELEN MIRREN

I AM A GREAT
BELIEVER IN LUCK.
THE HARDER I WORK,
THE MORE OF IT I
SEEM TO HAVE.

COLEMAN COX

EDUCATION IS THE KEY TO UNLOCKING THE WORLD, A PASSPORT TO FREEDOM.

OPRAH WINFREY

DREAM
BIG AND
WORK
HARD

BELIEVING IN YOURSELF IS
THE FIRST NECESSARY STEP
TO COMING EVEN CLOSE TO
ACHIEVING YOUR POTENTIAL.

SHERYL SANDBERG

EDUCATION IS THE MOST POWERFUL WEAPON WE CAN USE TO CHANGE THE WORLD.

NELSON MANDELA

YOUR HARD WORK HAS PAID OFF!

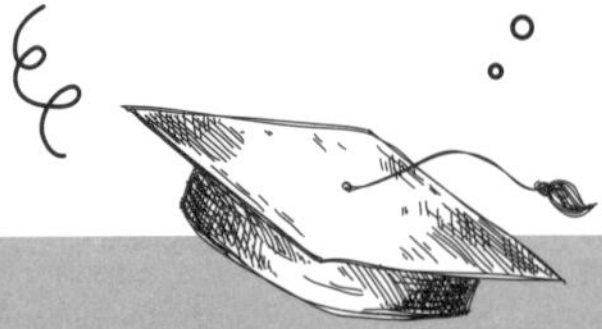

YOU CAN'T PUT A LIMIT ON ANYTHING. THE MORE YOU DREAM, THE FARTHER YOU GET.

MICHAEL PHELPS

IT'S ALWAYS
A GOOD MOVE TO
LISTEN TO THAT
INNER VOICE...
IF IT DOESN'T LEAD
TO A CRIME.

LISA KUDROW

WHEREVER YOU GO, GO WITH ALL YOUR HEART.

CONFUCIUS

The formula of happiness and success is just being actually yourself, in the most vivid possible way you can.

MERYL STREEP

ENJOY THE PROCESS OF YOUR SEARCH WITHOUT SUCCUMBING TO THE PRESSURE OF THE RESULT. TRUST YOUR GUT. KEEP THROWING DARTS AT THE DARTBOARD.

WILL FERRELL

TAKE PRIDE IN
HOW FAR YOU
HAVE COME.
HAVE FAITH
IN HOW FAR
YOU CAN GO.

THE FUTURE BELONGS TO THOSE WHO WORK HARD

DREAMS CAN CHANGE.
IF WE'D ALL STUCK WITH
OUR FIRST DREAM, THE WORLD
WOULD BE OVERRUN WITH
COWBOYS AND PRINCESSES.

STEPHEN COLBERT

THE ONLY
THING THAT EVER
SAT ITS WAY TO
SUCCESS WAS
A HEN.

SARAH BROWN

SUCCESS IS NOT THE KEY TO HAPPINESS. HAPPINESS IS THE KEY TO SUCCESS. IF YOU LOVE WHAT YOU ARE DOING, YOU WILL BE SUCCESSFUL.

ALBERT SCHWEITZER

Turn your
DREAMS
into plans

IF YOU CAN FIND A PATH WITH NO OBSTACLES, IT PROBABLY DOESN'T LEAD ANYWHERE.

FRANK A. CLARK

WHEN THE WHOLE WORLD IS SILENT, EVEN ONE VOICE BECOMES POWERFUL.

MALALA YOUSAFZAI

THE
BEST
IS YET
TO COME

EVEN IF
YOU ARE ON
THE RIGHT TRACK,
YOU WILL GET RUN
OVER IF YOU JUST
SIT THERE.

WILL ROGERS

TOMORROW'S ILLITERATE WILL NOT BE THE MAN WHO CAN'T READ; HE WILL BE THE MAN WHO HAS NOT LEARNED HOW TO LEARN.

HERBERT GERJUOY

THE MIND
IS NOT A VESSEL
TO BE FILLED,
BUT A FIRE TO
BE KINDLED.

PLUTARCH

DON'T LET PEOPLE WHO THINK TOO SMALL TELL YOU YOUR DREAMS ARE TOO BIG

You don't go to university so you can punch a clock. You go to university so you can be in a position to make a difference.

JANET NAPOLITANO

IF WE ALL DID THE THINGS THAT WE ARE CAPABLE OF DOING, WE WOULD LITERALLY ASTOUND OURSELVES.

THOMAS EDISON

IF YOU
LOSE FOCUS,
GET GLASSES

POWER'S NOT GIVEN TO YOU. YOU HAVE TO TAKE IT.

BEYONCÉ

LEARNING IS NOT THE PRODUCT OF TEACHING. LEARNING IS THE PRODUCT OF THE ACTIVITY OF LEARNERS.

JOHN HOLT

I HAVE
NEVER LET
MY SCHOOLING
INTERFERE
WITH MY
EDUCATION.

MARK TWAIN

TODAY IS
JUST THE FIRST
OF SO MANY
ACHIEVEMENTS

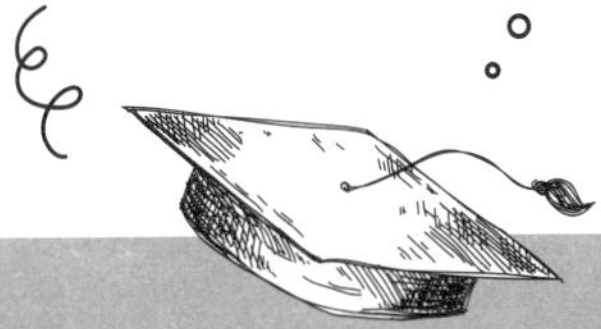

THE CHALLENGE IS
NOT TO BE PERFECT...
IT'S TO BE WHOLE.

JANE FONDA

BE BRAVE.
TAKE RISKS.
NOTHING CAN
SUBSTITUTE
EXPERIENCE.

PAUL COELHO

You SMASHED IT!

THERE MAY BE DAYS WHEN YOU'LL SAY TO YOURSELF, "I CAN'T. I LITERALLY CAN'T EVEN." BUT YOU CAN! YOU CAN EVEN!

KATIE COURIC

NOT ONLY
CAN YOU NOT
PLAN THE IMPACT
YOU'RE GOING TO
HAVE, YOU OFTEN
WON'T RECOGNIZE
IT WHEN YOU'RE
HAVING IT.

DICK COSTOLO

People become really quite remarkable when they start thinking that they can do things.

NORMAN VINCENT PEALE

IF YOU
ARE HAPPY,
YOU ARE
SUCCESSFUL

NEVER LET THE FEAR OF STRIKING OUT KEEP YOU FROM PLAYING THE GAME.

BABE RUTH

YOU NEVER SHOULD SPEND YOUR TIME BEING THE FORMER ANYTHING.

CONDOLEEZZA RICE

MAY THE
FRIENDS
YOU MADE
LAST LONGER
THAN YOUR
STUDENT DEBT

YOU CAN FAIL AT WHAT YOU DON'T WANT, SO YOU MIGHT AS WELL TAKE A CHANCE ON DOING WHAT YOU LOVE.

JIM CARREY

AND WILL
YOU SUCCEED?
YES! YOU WILL,
INDEED! (98 AND
¾ PER CENT
GUARANTEED.)

DR SEUSS

WHO QUESTIONS MUCH, SHALL LEARN MUCH, AND RETAIN MUCH.

FRANCIS BACON

IF YOU GET LOST ON YOUR WAY TO YOUR DREAMS, FIND A BETTER PATH

YOUR TIME
IS LIMITED, SO
DON'T WASTE IT
LIVING SOMEONE
ELSE'S LIFE.

STEVE JOBS

YOU CAN NEVER BE OVERDRESSED OR OVEREDUCATED.

OSCAR WILDE

NEVER
STOP PURSUING
KNOWLEDGE

THE
DIRECTION
IN WHICH
EDUCATION
STARTS A MAN
WILL DETERMINE
HIS FUTURE LIFE.

PLATO

If you hear a voice within you say "You cannot paint", then by all means paint and that voice will be silenced.

VINCENT VAN GOGH

EDUCATION'S
PURPOSE IS TO REPLACE
AN EMPTY MIND WITH
AN OPEN ONE.

MALCOLM FORBES

Totally

GRAD-ICAL

THE DICTIONARY IS THE ONLY PLACE WHERE SUCCESS COMES BEFORE WORK.

ANONYMOUS

THE ONLY THING YOU CAN DO IN THIS LIFE IS PURSUE YOUR PASSIONS, CELEBRATE YOUR BLOOPERS AND NEVER STOP FOLLOWING YOUR FEAR.

GRACE HELBIG

THE TASSEL WAS WORTH THE HASSLE

I ENCOURAGE YOU TO LIVE WITH LIFE. BE COURAGEOUS, ADVENTUROUS. GIVE US A TOMORROW, MORE THAN WE DESERVE.

MAYA ANGELOU

DEVELOP A PASSION FOR LEARNING. IF YOU DO, YOU WILL NEVER CEASE TO GROW.

ANTHONY J. D'ANGELO

WITHOUT
LABOR, NOTHING
PROSPERS.

SOPHOCLES

THE
BEST THINGS
COME TO THOSE
WHO DON'T
GIVE UP

LIFE IS TEN PER CENT WHAT HAPPENS TO YOU AND NINETY PER CENT HOW YOU RESPOND TO IT.

CHARLES SWINDOLL

SURE I AM
OF THIS, THAT
YOU HAVE ONLY
TO ENDURE TO
CONQUER.

WINSTON CHURCHILL

Make the most of yourself
by fanning the tiny, inner
sparks of possibility into
flames of achievement.

GOLDA MEIR

LET
THE ADVENTURE
BEGIN

LIFE IS MY COLLEGE. MAY I GRADUATE WELL, AND EARN SOME HONORS!

LOUISA MAY ALCOTT

GRADUATION
IS NOT AN END;
IT'S A BEGINNING.

ORRIN HATCH

TAKE CRITICISM SERIOUSLY, BUT NOT PERSONALLY. IF THERE IS TRUTH OR MERIT IN THE CRITICISM, TRY TO LEARN FROM IT. OTHERWISE, LET IT ROLL RIGHT OFF YOU.

HILLARY CLINTON

WHEN YOU LEAVE
HERE, DON'T FORGET
WHY YOU CAME.

ADLAI STEVENSON II

Congratulations
on your
GRADUATION!

Have you enjoyed this book? If so, find us on Facebook at **SUMMERSDALE PUBLISHERS**, on Twitter/X at **@SUMMERSDALE** and on Instagram and TikTok at **@SUMMERSDALEBOOKS** and get in touch. We'd love to hear from you!

WWW.SUMMERSDALE.COM

IMAGE CREDITS

pp.4, 16, 21, 29, 42, 53, 67, 79, 92, 105, 117, 130, 142, 158 © Gun2becontinued/Shutterstock.com
pp.3, 5, 12, 18, 30, 39, 43, 49, 56, 61, 68, 74, 81, 86, 93, 99, 106, 112, 119, 124, 131, 137, 144, 149, 156 © Artishok/Shutterstock.com
pp.9, 22, 35, 47, 60, 72, 85, 98, 109, 123, 135, 148 (cap) © Lina_Lisichka/Shutterstock.com
pp.9, 22, 35, 47, 60, 72, 85, 98, 109, 123, 135, 148 (twirl) © solarus/Shutterstock.com
pp.6, 24, 41, 59, 76, 94, 111, 129, 146 (mortarboard) © Arned Design/Shutterstock.com
pp.17, 34, 52, 66, 87, 104, 122, 136 © love pattern/Shutterstock.com
pp.13, 31, 48, 69, 80, 97, 118, 139, 154, 160 © cgterminal/Shutterstock.com
pp.8, 14, 20, 23, 26, 33, 36, 38, 46, 51, 55, 58, 64, 71, 73, 77, 84, 89, 90, 96, 100, 108, 110, 114, 121, 125, 127, 134, 140, 143, 147, 152, 155, 159 (sunburst) © Jason Winter/Shutterstock.com